# An Elephant
## in the
# Living Room

## The Children's Book

Jill M. Hastings, M.S.
Marion H. Typpo, Ph. D.
Illustrations by Mimi Noland

CompCare
Publishers

2415 Annapolis Lane, Minneapolis, Minnesota 55441

© 1984 by Jill M. Hastings, M.S. and Marion H. Typpo, Ph.D.
All rights reserved.
Published in the United States
by CompCare Publishers.

Reproduction in whole or part, in any form, including storage in memory
device system, is forbidden without written permission ... except that portions
may be used in broadcast or printed commentary or review when attributed
fully to author and publication by names.

Library of Congress Catalog Card Number 84-70189
ISBN 0-89638-071-8

Cover design by Kristen McDougall

Inquiries, orders, and catalog should be addressed to
CompCare Publishers
2415 Annapolis Lane
Minneapolis, Minnesota 55441
Call toll free 800/328-3330
(Minnesota residents 612/559-4800)

      8   9
91   92   93

This book is dedicated, with much love, to my family,

Mom, Dad, Tom, Mike, and Maureen,

and to

Betty and Bob Concannon

and

to

you!

# Acknowledgments

This book would not have been possible without the cooperation and encouragement of the staffs at the St. Mary's Rehabilitation Center in Minneapolis, Minnesota, and the Family Counseling Center in Columbia, Missouri,

and the following children and teenagers:

Mandy, Gil, Matt, Lisa, Caryn, Melissa, Gib, Becca, Shawn, Mark, Renee, Tim, Tom, Tara, Denise, Ryan, Tricia, Tracy, Liz, Shari, Judy, Darcy, Preston, Terri, Penny, Mary, Shuana, Lee, Eric, Dan, Kathy, Mary, Diane, Lori, Barry, Chris, Kelly, Tim, Della, Jared, Greg, Stephanie, Laura, Jessica, Daren, Jeff, Mike, Chris, Scott, Andy, Lee, Jody, Linda, Terry, Steve, Tricia, Tim, Karen, Betsy, Mindy, Louise, Ted, Debbie, Jim, Dave, Jerry, Greg, Lisa, James, Lee, Lennie, Anna, Gary, Julie, Gordon, Mike, Marty, Vince, Carolyn, Laura, Michelle, Paul, James, Tim, Pat, Nanci, Scott, Art, Randy, Greta, Paula, Chris, Jim, Theresa, Troy, Jason, Kiersa, Matt, Adam, Missy, and Michelle.

# An Elephant in the Living Room

Imagine an ordinary living room. . .chairs, couch, coffee table, a TV set and, in the middle, a

## LARGE, GRAY ELEPHANT.

The ELEPHANT stands there, shifting from one foot to another and slowly swaying from side to side.

Imagine also the people that live in this house; you, along with your mother and father and maybe some sisters and brothers. People have to go through the living room many times a day and you watch as they walk through it very. . . carefully. . .around. . .the. . .ELEPHANT. No one ever says anything about the ELEPHANT. They avoid the swinging trunk and just walk around it. Since no one ever talks about the ELEPHANT, you know that you're not supposed to talk about it either. And you don't.

But sometimes you wonder why nobody is saying anything or why no one is doing anything to move the ELEPHANT. After all, it's a very big elephant and it's very hard to keep walking around it all the time and people are getting very tired. You wonder if maybe there is something wrong with you. But you just keep wondering, keep walking around it, keep worrying and wishing that there was somebody to talk to about the ELEPHANT.

Living in a family where drinking is a problem is a lot like living with an ELEPHANT in the living room. This book is a way to begin talking about things that are hard to talk about.

# Introduction

When I was about ten years old, I started to realize that my dad had a drinking problem. Sometimes he drank too much. Then he would talk loudly and make jokes that weren't funny. He would say unkind things to my mom in front of the neighbors and my friends. I felt embarrassed.

Sometimes I tried to control how much he drank. He would ask me to make him a drink, and I would "forget" on purpose to put the alcohol in it. I hoped he wouldn't notice, but he always did. Then he'd get angry. His drinks were very important to him. Sometimes I felt his drinking was more important to him than I was. He would start drinking at a bar after work, and he would forget to come home until late at night. I worried that he might drive drunk and crash his car and not make it home at all. I knew Mom worried too. Sometimes she and Dad would have loud quarrels. I was scared they might get divorced. Then what would happen to my brothers and sister and me?

Besides the bad times, there were lots of good times too. My dad would tell us great bedtime stories. He coached my brothers' baseball teams. We took vacations to the lakes and to my grandparents' house. He sent me flowers when I was in the school play. Sometimes he was a really good dad to have around.

I guess that's why I was confused a lot. Sometimes I loved him, and sometimes I was so angry at him I thought I hated him. My feelings went up and down. I felt as if I lived on a roller coaster. I was never quite sure what would happen next at my house.

Finally, I worried so much that I went to see a counselor. This counselor knew a lot about feelings, and about people with drinking and drug problems. He told me that my dad's drinking was not my fault. He helped me understand that I couldn't control my dad's drinking, no matter how hard I tried. With this counselor's help, I realized that I couldn't make my dad change, but I could change my own life. The counselor encouraged me to join a group of other people who met to talk about their problems and their feelings. In this group, I learned how to handle my feelings and how to make some changes in my life that helped me feel happier and better about myself.

Eventually the rest of my family got help too. My mom started to go to Al-Anon, a group that helps people who live in alcoholic families. My father finally decided to go to a special hospital for people with drinking and other drug problems. While he was in the hospital, my whole family went there often to learn about his sickness of alcoholism — and to have family counseling that helped us understand alcoholism and how to get along better as a family.

Now I am grown up. I have lots of friends, and I am happy with my life. Coping with my family's problems helped me learn to face my own problems and to understand my feelings. Because of what I learned in counseling, in discussion groups, and through reading, I am a more caring, sensitive, and happier person.

But I still remember the confusion and loneliness I felt while I was growing up in a family where drinking was a problem. That's why I decided to write this book.

To write this book, I first met in small groups with over one hundred kids and teenagers who lived in families where drinking and drug use is a problem. They shared their feelings and suggestions in hopes that it would help others. They wanted other kids to know that they were not alone with their problems, and that, with help, life can be better.

You may be reading this book with a group of other kids who have people in their families who have drinking problems. Or you may be reading this book with an adult who cares about you. Either way, it is your book. There are spaces and pages for you to write or draw if you want to. This is not a school book. There are no right or wrong answers. You don't need to worry about spelling things correctly. If you want to share your answers, you may. If you want to keep them private, that is okay, too.

All of us who worked on this book hope that it will help you understand alcoholism as a disease, learn new ways to handle your feelings, and learn to like yourself better. We wish for you the freedom to grow and to enjoy your life.


Jill Hastings

Dear Parents,

This book was written for children age seven through early adolescence who are living in families where drinking or drug use is or has been a problem. Living in a family where this is a problem can be painful and confusing at times. Usually all members, including the drinker, are doing the best they can to survive the pain and confusion. Sometimes we adults cope by denying the problem. Sometimes our children do the same. But pain, when it is recognized, understood, and dealt with directly, can motivate us to learn better ways of living and loving.

The children in these families are often silent sufferers who do not appear to be affected. Yet without help they are more likely than their peers to develop drinking or other drug problems themselves, or to marry people who do. These children are also more likely to develop emotional and social adjustment problems in childhood and adulthood.

So, even though our children may be silent about their suffering, they are affected by this disease. The activities in this book are designed to help children:

1. Improve their relationships with parents and siblings.
2. Learn to recognize their feelings and express them appropriately.
3. Improve their self-esteem by recognizing their strengths and abilities.
4. Develop some practical ways of coping with some common problems in families where there is drinking or drug misuse.
5. Understand that addiction to alcohol or other drugs is a disease and that they are not the cause of this disease.
6. Realize that they are not alone—that other children are coping with similar problems.

*The children's book* is designed to be read aloud and shared with a child or group of children by a counselor or other adult who has knowledge about working with children from families where drinking or other drug use is a problem.

We invite you to look through the book. If you have concerns or questions about it, please talk with the adult who will be helping your child with the book's activities. We would also welcome any suggestions you have. Please write to us in care of the publisher.

Sincerely,

Jill Hastings and Marion Typpo

# Keeping Confidences

When we are confident in someone, we trust that person to understand what we are saying and feeling. We trust that person to respect our opinions and feelings.

While you are reading this book, you may share your feelings with other kids in your group. Others will probably share their feelings with you.

It is important to remember that everybody owns his or her own feelings. That's why we have the rule "Don't tell anybody outside the group what someone else says in the group." It is not fair to tell someone else's feelings because those are his or her feelings, not yours.

Also, when we are confident in someone, we trust that person to understand what we mean. It is a sad thing, but many people do not understand about alcoholism. They do not know that alcoholism is a sickness. In fact, most alcoholics themselves do not understand this. If someone were to tell them they were alcoholic, they would get angry and embarrassed. They do not believe that they are alcoholic. They do not understand about alcoholism.

That is another reason why things said in the group should stay in the group. It is not a good idea to talk outside the group about another child's drinking parent. That parent might not understand about alcoholism and, if he or she heard what was said, might get really angry at the child. The child would probably feel hurt that someone in the group did not keep the confidence.

For group leaders, there is an exception to this rule. Sometimes a child is physically or emotionally hurt by an adult. When that happens and the child tells about it here, the leader has a responsibility by law to report it to the agency in charge of protecting children. All children deserve to be protected.

In general, the rule is:

"Don't tell other people outside the group about things that someone else said in the group".

We will keep each others' confidences. We will trust each other.

# About Our Group

If you are doing this in a group, you may want to fill in this page:

My name is _____

and I like _____

and _____

and _____

_____ .

The first names of the other kids in my group are:

_____     _____

_____     _____

_____     _____

_____     _____

_____     _____

We meet on _____

at _____

Our leaders' names are _____

and _____ .

# Rules of Our Group

1. Only one person talks at a time.

2. Pay attention to the person who is talking. Don't interrupt.

3. Don't tell people outside the group about what someone else says in the group. We will keep each other's confidences. (Be sure to read "Keeping Confidences.")

4. Don't put each other down. Don't say things to each other in a way that tells somebody that he or she is dumb, stupid, crazy, or ugly. No teasing.

5. Nobody will make anybody talk or write or draw. If someone chooses not to answer a question or do an activity, that is okay.

6. If I choose not to talk or do an activity, I will sit quietly and pay attention to the others.

7. _____
   _____ .

8. _____
   _____
   _____ .

I agree to these rules.


_____
(Sign your name here)


_____
(Date)

# Contents

# 1
# Drinking and Drug Problems

A drug is something we put into our body that changes how our body works. Aspirin, penicillin, alcohol, and marijuana are names of some drugs. All drugs affect our body in some way. Some drugs affect how we think. Some drugs, like penicillin, affect how our body heals itself.

Other drugs affect our moods (feelings). Drugs that affect our feelings are called mood-changing drugs. Alcohol and marijuana are drugs that change our moods. The names of some drugs are listed below. Circle the drugs that can change a person's moods.

| | | |
|---|---|---|
| **Aspirin** | **Penicillin** | **Librium** |
| **Nicotine** | **Heroin** | **Valium** |
| **Marijuana** | | **Alcohol** |

## Can you guess?

1. A mood-changing drug found in beer, wine, and liquors (like whiskey, scotch, bourbon, and vodka) is called _____ .

2. "Pot" is a nickname for the mood-changing drug _____ .

3.	Some pills that change people's moods are _____

and _____ .

Drinking alcohol or using other mood-changing drugs changes how people act. Think of a time you saw someone drunk or high. Circle the words below that describe how they acted (you can add your own words too):

**Fell asleep**            **Got clumsy**            **Said something stupid**

**Got mad**                **Acted scary**            **Did something crazy**

**Yelled**                 _____          _____

_____          _____          _____

Sometimes people are not careful when they are drinking or using other drugs. Joe's father drank one beer after another, until he drank too much and drove the car into a tree. Peter's mom drank too much and did silly things that embarrassed Peter in front of his friends. Susan's mother took lots of pills. The pills made her forget about the time. She forgot to fix dinner.

People who use too much of a mood-changing drug—like alcohol or marijuana—become "drunk" or "high." They cannot think clearly. They forget things. Their bodies do not work as well. They do clumsy or silly things. Sometimes they say crazy things or see things that aren't really there. People who are drunk or high can lose control of their thinking, their feelings, and their actions. Being around someone who is drunk or high can feel scary.

Think of a time you were around someone who was drunk or high and you felt embarrassed or afraid. Try to write about that time here:

When he was drunk, he _____

and I felt _____ .

When she was drunk, she _____

and I felt _____ .

People who drink or use other mood-changing drugs, even when it keeps causing problems with family, work, or health, are sick. They have a disease called "alcoholism" or "chemical dependency." The sickness is the same whether a person uses alcohol or other drugs. In this book we will call this disease alcoholism, although the person may be using other drugs.

People who keep drinking (or using drugs) even when it keeps causing problems are usually <u>addicted</u>. Addicted means stuck. They are stuck to drinking and

2

using drugs, just like you need to scratch when you itch. People who are addicted to alcohol or other drugs need help to quit drinking or using drugs. They cannot do it on their own. They are sick. We call people with this sickness "alcoholics."

Before I learned about alcoholism, I thought that alcoholics were grungy, dirty old men who lay in gutters and had wine bottles hanging out their ears.

What do you think an alcoholic looks like? Draw it here:

Most alcoholics are just regular people. Alcoholics can be men or women, boys or girls, rich or poor, tall or short, fat or thin. Alcoholics work as doctors, dentists, construction workers, teachers, mechanics, grocery store clerks, and in many other kinds of jobs.

**Every alcoholic is somebody's mother, father, sister, brother, or friend.**

Do you think somebody in your family might have this sickness of alcoholism?

_____

What happens to make you think that? _____

_____

_____

_____

Here are some questions that might help you figure out if you have a problem with a drinking parent:*

1. Do you worry about your mom's or dad's drinking?  YES  NO
2. Do you sometimes feel that you are the reason your parents drink so much? YES  NO
3. Are you ashamed to have your friends come to your house and are you finding more and more excuses to stay away from home?  YES  NO
4. Do you sometimes feel as though you hate your parents when they are drinking and then feel guilty for hating them?  YES  NO
5. Have you been watching how much your parent drinks?  YES  NO
6. Do you try to make your parents happy so they won't get upset and drink more?  YES  NO
7. Do you feel you can't talk about the drinking in your home—or even how you feel inside?  YES  NO
8. Do you sometimes take drugs to forget about things at home?  YES  NO
9. Do you feel if your parents really loved you they wouldn't drink so much? YES  NO
10. Do you sometimes wish you had never been born?  YES  NO
11. Do you want to start feeling better?  YES  NO

If you answered yes to some of these questions, you may have a parent with a drinking problem. This book can help you learn more about alcoholism. One way to help yourself start feeling better is to learn about what alcoholism really is.

*These questions are from a very good booklet by a daughter of alcoholic parents: *The Secret Everyone Knows* by Cathleen Brooks. (Hazelden Educational Materials, Center City, Minnesota.)

## Alcoholism is a sickness, but you can't catch it.

Alcoholism isn't caused by a germ. In fact, no one knows for sure what causes alcoholism. It does seem to happen more often in some families than in others. For instance, John's dad, grandpa, and aunt all are alcoholics. Scientists and doctors don't know why this is so. Maybe some people's bodies are more sensitive to alcohol and other mood-changing drugs. Or maybe if people grow up in a family where they see alcohol used to change feelings, they learn to follow that example. No one knows for sure why alcoholism happens again and again in some families. Doctors and scientists are trying to find out.

One thing we do know: You can't cause someone to become an alcoholic. IT'S NOT YOUR FAULT. But sometimes kids think it is their fault.

Janice, who is ten, thought maybe she caused her dad's drinking problem. She says, "I used to make him drinks when he told me to. Maybe I caused him to be an alcoholic." But she didn't. You can't make somebody become an alcoholic.

Barb sometimes blames her mom's drinking problem on herself. She says, "Sometimes I think maybe if I got better grades in school, or if I was prettier, or if I worked harder to keep my room clean, then maybe my mom would be happy and not drink so much." But it's not Barb's fault. Even if a fairy godmother came along and made Barb prettier, smarter, or neater...her mom would still drink too much. She would still be an alcoholic. She is sick and needs help to stop drinking.

People who are sick with alcoholism cannot stop drinking for very long unless they get help from a counselor or a doctor who understands alcoholism, an Alcoholics Anonymous (AA) group, or a treatment center.

Barb's mother tried to quit drinking several times. Sometimes she would stop drinking for several weeks. Barb would think everything was going to be okay. Then something would happen and her mom would start drinking again. Barb would try very hard to keep her mom from drinking. She even hid her mom's beer. But nothing worked. Her mom always started drinking again.

YOU CANNOT CONTROL AN ALCOHOLIC'S DRINKING. YOU CANNOT STOP AN ALCOHOLIC FROM DRINKING. Alcoholism is a disease. Alcoholics need specially trained people to help them get well.

Did you ever feel as if your parent's (or brother's or sister's) drinking problem was your fault? _____ .


If you did feel it was your fault, what happened to make you think that?

_____

_____ .

## Alcoholism: A 'feelings' disease.

People who are alcoholic have trouble with their feelings. When they have uncomfortable feelings and don't know how to handle them, they drink (or use other drugs) to change those feelings. An alcoholic uses drinking to change uncomfortable feelings. But using drinking to change feelings doesn't work very well. It usually causes more problems—with family, friends, job, or health. Drinking to change feelings is not a good way to handle feelings. In this book, we will learn some better ways to handle feelings.

## One more time, since these are important to remember:
1. All drugs affect your body in some way.
2. Alcohol (like beer, wine, and scotch), marijuana, Valium, Librium, and heroin are drugs that change a person's feelings. They are mood-changing drugs.

3. Drinking or using a mood-changing drug can make a person "drunk" or "high". People do not think clearly when drunk or high. They may say and do silly or hurtful things that they don't mean.

4. People who use alcohol or other drugs, even when their alcohol or drug use keeps causing problems at home or in their families or at work, are sick. We say they are <u>alcoholic</u> or <u>chemically dependent</u>. They <u>depend</u> on alcohol or other mood-changing drugs to try to feel better.

5. Alcoholism is a sickness that many people have.

6. Alcoholism is not catching.

7. You can't make someone alcoholic. A person's alcoholism <u>is not your fault</u>.

8. You can't make someone stop drinking.

9. An alcoholic <u>must</u> get help to stop drinking — from an AA group, doctor, counselor, or special hospital that treats alcoholics.

10. Alcoholism is a "feelings" disease.

11. Drinking to change uncomfortable feelings is not a good way to handle feelings.

Here are some other books about alcohol and alcoholism. You can ask your librarian to help you find them. Or look in the Suggested Reading list on page 64 to find out.

*Living with a Parent Who Drinks Too Much* by Judith Seixas

*Alcohol: What It Is, What It Does* by Judith Seixas

*First Step* by Anne Snyder

*Pot: What It Is, What It Does* by Anne Tobias

*What's Drunk, Mama?* by Al-Anon Family Groups.

# 2

See if you can guess what I'm thinking of. Here are some clues: Everyone in the whole world has them. They can make your body feel tense and tight, or loose and floppy and jittery. They make people laugh and cry. Some of them are comfortable, and some are uncomfortable. They can help us understand ourselves and our wants and needs. We can share them with other people, or we can keep them wrapped up inside ourselves. Without them, life would be boring.

What do you think these are? _____

Did you guess feelings? Everyone in the whole world has feelings. Some feelings, like anger, can make your body feel tense and tight. Some feelings, like happiness, can make your body feel loose and floppy and relaxed. Some feelings, like nervousness, make your body feel jittery. Some feelings are comfortable (happiness, excitement, love) and some are uncomfortable (anger, fear, embarrassment).

Some people share their feelings with other people. Some people try to hold all their feelings inside, or try to pretend they are not there.

The following story is a make-believe story, but it has something important to say about handling feelings. See if you can figure out what it is trying to tell us about a good way to handle feelings.

# Fuzzy's Feelings

Once upon a time there was a red, white, and blue caterpillar named Fuzzy Henry. Fuzzy loved to crawl through the grass, stretching his long body in the warm sun. Sometimes he and his friends would crawl to their special clubhouse under the tree roots. They'd tell jokes for hours. Fuzzy would feel loose and relaxed, enjoying the laughter rippling through his body. Other times Fuzzy felt brave and proud as he wore his yellow safety patrol belt when he helped the younger caterpillars cross the street for school. Sometimes at night, when Fuzzy's mom hugged him and tucked him into his warm, safe bed, Fuzzy let all the warm, happy feelings float through his body as he drifted off to sleep. Fuzzy enjoyed all those comfortable, warm, happy feelings. He let them come and go easily.

But sometimes Fuzzy had a not-so-comfortable feeling. One day Fuzzy got an F on his math test. He felt embarrassed and ashamed. He didn't know what to do with these feelings. Fuzzy swallowed them down and tried to pretend they weren't there. Besides, he thought, there were more pleasant things to think about. Today was his birthday. Fuzzy's dad had promised to come home right after work in time for Fuzzy's special birthday dinner.

After school, Fuzzy hurried home. He couldn't crawl fast though, because his body was heavy with the embarrassment and fear he had swallowed down. Butch, one of his classmates, noticed how much slower Fuzzy was moving. He yelled to the rest of the caterpillars, "Look at Fuzzy, he can't even keep up. Besides being stupid in math, he is as slow as molasses." Fuzzy felt so embarrassed he wanted to hide. And he felt so angry at Butch he wanted to punch him. But instead, Fuzzy just swallowed his angry, embarrassed feelings. He started to feel like he was pulling a weight behind him. He thought, "It doesn't matter, I'll be home soon, Dad will be there, and Mom will have my birthday dinner ready. Everything will be wonderful!"

Fuzzy crawled up the steps and into the house. "Hey Dad, hey Mom, I'm home!" But the house was dark and quiet. All he could hear were sounds of someone crying in his parents' bedroom. He opened the door and saw his mom crying on the bed. He guessed his dad and mom had been fighting again. He quietly closed the door and crawled downstairs to his dad's workroom. He heard his dad's drunken voice inside. His dad sat at the workbench with empty bottles of beer scattered around him. His dad saw him, but he didn't even say happy birthday. Disgusted and angry, Fuzzy slammed the door and scrambled upstairs and out of the house.

He climbed a tree and crawled out on the limb to a large leaf. He was so angry at his dad. Dad had promised it would be a good birthday! He had promised he wouldn't drink today. Fuzzy tried to swallow his hurt and angry feelings. But there wasn't any room left inside. So instead, all the angry, frustrated, and hurt feelings stuck to the outside of his furry body. Soon, the uncomfortable feelings formed a stiff cocoon around him. He couldn't see out. It was dark and lonely being stuck inside the cocoon. Fuzzy felt scared. He didn't know what to do. He couldn't even move, stuck inside the dark cocoon.

Suddenly Fuzzy felt the leaf bounce up and down. He heard the flappings of wings outside the cocoon. Something was yelling, "Hey, is anybody in there?"

"Yes, yes. I'm in here," yelled Fuzzy.

"Well, who are you?" yelled the voice.

"I'm Fuzzy the caterpillar. It's dark and lonely in here and I'm scared. Please get me out!" Fuzzy yelled back.

Just then, a piece of cocoon chipped off. A shaft of light shone in. Fuzzy could see part of the wing of a butterfly. "Who — are you?" asked Fuzzy.

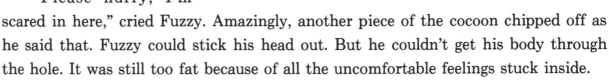

"I'm RAS, a butterfly," said a voice that must have been connected to the yellow wings. "Are you stuck in there?"

"Yes," yelled Fuzzy. "Please get me out."

"Please hurry, I'm scared in here," cried Fuzzy. Amazingly, another piece of the cocoon chipped off as he said that. Fuzzy could stick his head out. But he couldn't get his body through the hole. It was still too fat because of all the uncomfortable feelings stuck inside.

RAS flew around the cocoon, inspecting it. He stuck part of his antennae into the cocoon. Then he landed on the leaf, right in front of Fuzzy's head. "I can't get you out," said RAS. "But I can show you how to get out."

"Good. How?" asked Fuzzy.

RAS replied, "Well, first you are going to have to let go of some of those uncomfortable feelings. You've got so many locked up inside of you you're stuck."

"But how do I let them out?" asked Fuzzy.

"I'll give you a hint," said RAS. "Think of the letters of my name — R-A-S. R stands for recognize your feelings. Realize what you are holding inside. For example, how did you feel when you got an F on your math test?"

"I felt embarrassed and ashamed. And when Butch made fun of me, I felt so angry I wanted to hit him. Then when I got home and dad was drunk, I felt mad and hurt that he broke his promise about not drinking on my birthday."

"See. You can recognize your feelings," said RAS. "Next, you need to accept them."

"What do you mean by that?" asked Fuzzy.

"I mean that it helps to understand that everybody has feelings. Feelings aren't right or wrong, they just <u>are</u>. Some feel comfortable, some don't. But the more you try to stuff and hide the uncomfortable feelings inside, the worse you feel. You'll be stuck inside that dark and lonely cocoon forever. It helps to learn to <u>share</u> your feelings. It's usually best to share your feelings with the person you're having the feelings about."

"But what can I do?" cried Fuzzy. "If I get mad and punch Butch, he'll pound me into the ground. I can't tell my mom I feel hurt when she's already crying. And right now my dad's too drunk to care."

"Yes, I'd say you've got a problem. Let's take Butch first. Instead of saying 'Butch, you're a dirty rotten creep and you make me mad!' You could say instead, 'Butch, I already feel bad about my math test. When you make fun of me, I feel worse.' "

"What if he laughs at me when I say that?" said Fuzzy.

"Then I think you don't need him. Go find some more understanding friends!"

"Okay," said Fuzzy. "But what do I do about my feelings about my dad? He's too drunk to talk to. I might get hit."

"It's not a good idea to share your feelings with someone who is drunk," agreed RAS. "Drunk people aren't in control of themselves. They might do something dangerous or crazy. Maybe there is someone else you can share your feelings with."

"Well, sometimes I can share them with my mom. But right now she's all upset and crying. I'm not even sure she'd hear me," said Fuzzy.

"Lot's of times having a good friend to share with can help," said RAS.

"You mean, a friend like you?" asked Fuzzy.

"Sure," smiled RAS. "If I'm not around, you can find others. How about your basketball coach? Or your friend Pete's mom? Or a favorite teacher? Or the counselor at school? There are lots of people who would listen if you let them know it is important to you."

"But it's hard to get started," said Fuzzy. "I mean, it's pretty embarrassing stuff to talk about. What if they don't understand about my dad's drinking?"

"Then you keep trying until you find someone who <u>does</u> understand. You're right, it isn't easy. But would you rather stay stuck in that lonely cocoon? Or get headaches and stomachaches from keeping those feelings all stuck inside?" asked RAS. "Besides, even when you can't find someone to talk to right away, you can let out your feelings in other ways. Some people write them down in a notebook. Some talk to a pet dog or cat. One guy I know has a friendly tree he talks to. There are lots of ways to share feelings."

Fuzzy looked thoughtful. "But I've had all those feelings inside for so long. What if I let them out all at once?" He imagined this big, scary explosion!

RAS smiled. "Lots of people feel scared about sharing feelings. Like you, they worry about exploding and scattering their feelings everywhere. But you don't have to explode with feelings. You <u>can</u> let them out a little at a time—whenever the time seems right."

"Gee," said Fuzzy, "talking to you has really felt good. Realizing my feelings, accepting them, and sharing them feels good, too. But getting started is hard."

14

Just then another part of the cocoon cracked open. Fuzzy poked his head out and yelled at RAS, "I think I can get out." Fuzzy struggled and pushed as RAS watched and cheered for his friend.

"Ouch, it hurts," cried Fuzzy, but he didn't stop. He kept pushing, and finally he was free! He started to shake out his body. Suddenly he noticed his fur was gone! In its place were lovely, long, thin, shining wings.

"Oh, RAS," he cried, "I'm like you! I'm a butterfly. I can fly!" With that Fuzzy fluttered his wings, raced up into the sky, and flew excitedly in circles around RAS.

Happily, RAS watched his friend flying around and around in circles. A spring breeze shook the leaf. RAS watched as the broken bits of cocoon fell to the ground. "Wings really are better then being trapped in a cocoon," thought RAS. Then he flipped his own wings, and flew up into the sky to join Fuzzy.

## Questions

Did you ever feel embarrassed and angry like Fuzzy? _____ .

What did you do with those feelings? _____

_____ .

What does RAS tell Fuzzy to do with his feelings? _____

_____ .

Do you think this is a good idea? _____ .

Why or why not? _____

_____ .

## Some feelings

Here is a list of feelings some kids made up. Can you think of some to add? Go ahead and write them below:

| | |
|---|---|
| sad | mad |
| embarrassed | nervous |
| happy | hopeless |
| scared | loving |
| miserable | caring |
| glad | grateful |
| hurt | excited |
| worried | warm |
| silly | strong |
| confused | frustrated |
| brave | loved |

_____     _____

_____     _____

_____     _____

Put a circle around the comfortable feelings.

# My feelings

Today I feel _____

_____ .

I feel happy when _____

_____ .

I feel sad when _____

_____ .

I feel angry when _____

_____ .

I feel important when _____

_____ .

I feel confused when _____

_____ .

I feel loved when _____

_____ .

I feel comfortable when _____

_____ .

I feel worried when _____

_____ .

I feel special when _____

_____ .

I feel hurt when _____

_____ .

I feel bad when _____

_____ .

I feel good when _____

_____ .

Can you think of some people you can share your feelings with? _____

Write their names here:

_____    _____


_____    _____

### Fuzzy's defenses

One day RAS and Fuzzy were flying around, practicing their flight patterns. They stopped to rest. "You know," said Fuzzy, "I feel better now that I can share my feelings. I didn't like being stuck in that dark cocoon. But there are some times when I don't want to share my feelings. And there are some people I don't want to share my feelings with. If I don't share my feelings, will I end up stuck in that lonely cocoon again?"

"Nobody shares all their feelings all the time," answered RAS. "There are some times when it is best not to share your feelings."

"Like when my dad is drunk?" asked Fuzzy.

"Yes. It doesn't usually help to share your feelings with your dad while he is drunk. He may not be able to comfort you or understand your feelings when he is drunk."

"I know that," said Fuzzy. "I tried telling my dad things when he's drunk, but by the next day he didn't even remember what I said."

"Yes, that happens, too, sometimes. It's called a blackout. It's when an alcoholic is drinking and talking and doing things, but the next day he or she can't remember a lot of what happened," explained RAS.

"Sometimes I'm still mad at my dad for the things he did or said while he was drinking the night before. Do you mean that sometimes he doesn't even remember those things?" asked Fuzzy.

"Probably not," replied RAS.

"RAS, what do you do when you don't want to share your feelings?" asked Fuzzy.

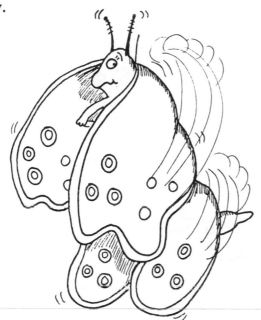

"When I choose not to share a feeling with someone, I close my wing over it. It's true that some people aren't very understanding sometimes, so I just don't bother sharing my feelings with them."

"Do you mean people like that bully, Butch? I shared my hurt feelings with him and he laughed at me. That hurt even more!" said Fuzzy. "But I didn't let him know he hurt me. I just smiled and walked away!"

"You were using your defenses," said RAS. "We use defenses such as walking away, or smiling on the outside when inside we feel hurt—to protect our feelings from getting hurt. Sometimes we need to use our defenses. But if we use our defenses <u>all</u> the time, no one knows how we really feel, or what we need. That's when we end up stuck in the cocoon."

"So you are telling me that it is a good idea to use defenses sometimes and with some people, as long as I don't hide behind the defenses all the time, right?" asked Fuzzy.

"That's right," RAS answered. "Come on. Let's go finish practicing our flight patterns now."

## Your Defenses

How do you protect your feelings sometimes? What do you look like when you are using your defenses? What do you do or say?

When I am mad, but I don't want somebody to know, I look like this

and I _____ .
(write what you do or say here)

When I am sad, but I don't want somebody to know, I look like this

and I _____ .
(write what you do or say here)

When I am happy, but I don't want somebody to know, I look like this

and I _____ .
(write what you do or say here)

When I am worried, but I don't want somebody to know, I look like this

and I _____ .
(write what you do or say here)

When my feelings hurt, but I don't want them to show, I look like this

and I _____ .
(write what you do or say here)

When I am scared, but I don't want somebody to know, I look like this

and I _____ .
(write what you do or say here)

## One more time, since these are important:

1. Every person in the world has feelings.
2. Feelings are not right or wrong. They just <u>are</u>.
3. Some feelings are comfortable, some feelings are uncomfortable.
4. It helps to recognize, accept, and share your feelings.
5. Sharing feelings can help us feel less lonely and afraid.
6. There are lots of ways to share feelings. You can talk to a friend, parent, teacher, or counselor. Or you can write them down and share them.
7. Sometimes we use defenses—such as ignoring, or smiling on the outside when inside we feel hurt.
8. We use defenses to protect our feelings from being hurt.
9. Sometimes we need to use our defenses.
10. If we use our defenses <u>all</u> the time, no one knows how we really feel, or what we need. It is good to find people we trust to share our feelings with.
11. When an alcoholic cannot remember what happened while he or she was drinking, it is called a blackout.

Here are some other books about feelings that you might want to read:

*What Makes Me Feel This Way?* by Eda LeShan

*You and Your Feelings* by Eda LeShan

*My Dad Loves Me, My Dad Has A Disease* by Claudia Black

*Handling Your Ups and Downs* by Joy Wilt

(Look in the back of this book under Suggested Reading to find out how to order these books.)

# 3
# Families

"I can never count on my mom," says Jean, who is 10. "Some days, she is fine. She cleans the house and fixes dinner and tells us funny bedtime stories. On other days she starts drinking in the morning and drinks all day long. By the time I get home from school, she is asleep on the couch. We can't even wake her up for dinner. She forgets all about us. I wish I lived in my friend Susan's family. Her mom bakes cookies, makes Susan's clothes, and teaches her to play the piano. It seems like Susan's family never has any problems."

1.  Did you ever feel that your family was the only family that had problems? ___ .

2.  Did you ever wish you lived in some other family? _____

What kind of family would you like to live in? _____

_____

Sometimes we feel that other families don't have problems like ours. We feel that way because we don't really know what is going on in these families. If families lived in glass houses and we could see what was happening in other families, we

22

would see that all families have problems. They might have <u>different</u> problems than your family, but <u>all</u> families have problems.

Learning to handle problems in a good way helps family members to grow and to be closer to each other.

Every family is different in some ways. For instance, every family has different members. Some families are large, others are small. On this page, draw a picture of your family.

# Family rules

Different families have different rules. What are some of the rules in your family?
Write them under the headings below.

Things I need to do: _____

_____

_____

_____

_____

_____

_____

_____

Things I should not do: _____

_____

_____

_____

_____

_____

_____

_____

_____

Most families have rules that everybody in the family knows, even though they may not talk about these rules. For example, "Don't tell Grandma about Dad's drinking." What are some of your family's unspoken rules? Write them here, if you want to:

_____

_____

_____

Sometimes, living in a family where drinking is a problem can be confusing. Shauna, thirteen, wrote: "My family has a problem it can't solve, and it's making everybody kinda crazy." Do (Did) you ever feel that way? _____

The reason things seem confusing is that feelings get all mixed up. When my dad was drinking, he would argue and say ugly things to my mom or brothers. I would feel so angry at him that I thought I hated him. Other times, when he was kind and funny and tried so hard to take care of us, I knew I loved him. It was confusing, loving and hating the same person. Did you ever feel that way?

_____

What did you do about these confusing feelings? (Circle the ones that apply to you, or add your own.)

                  Talked to someone about my feelings.
                  Held my feelings inside.
                  Pretended my feelings weren't there.
                  Wrote them down.
                  Got mad at _____ .

_____

_____

_____

Most of the time it helps to talk to someone you trust about your confusing feelings. Maybe you can talk to a favorite teacher, neighbor, or counselor. These people may be able to help you understand that your confusing feelings are natural. Talking about feelings can help you feel better. Think of some people you could talk to that might help you understand your confusing feelings. Write their names here:

_____

_____

Sometimes the people you talk to might not understand about alcoholism. Maybe you can share this book with them. It could help them understand about alcoholism and about your feelings too. Talk with the adult who is reading this book with you. Together you can decide whom to share this book with.

Sometimes the people who could understand and with whom we could share our feelings are right under our nose. Can you guess the missing words in this riddle?

Someone might live with you
With the same last name, too.
It's not your mom or dad or even yet
Your dog or cat or other pet.
Still, it's someone you always knew.
Sometimes they're a bother
Sometimes they're a pester
They are better known
As a _____
or _____ .

Did you guess brother or sister?

26

Do you have any brothers or sisters? Write their names and ages below:

Name _____     Age _____

Name _____     Age _____

Name _____     Age _____

Name _____     Age _____

Put a checkmark ___✔___ by the sentences with which you agree. Leave the others blank. Add your own if you want.

## I like having brothers and sisters because:

_____ it makes things more interesting.

_____ it makes things more fun sometimes.

_____ then I am not so lonely.

_____ sometimes they help me.

_____ then I have someone to play with.

_____ _____.

_____ _____.

## I don't like having brothers and sisters because:

_____ I have to share mom's and dad's attention with them and I want mom and dad all to myself sometimes.

_____ they borrow my stuff and don't take care of it.

_____ they tease me.

_____ they pick on me.

_____ they fight with me.

_____ they tell on me.

_____ they embarrass me.

_____ _____.

If you can, compare your list to your brother's and sister's.

Did you check some of the same things? _____

Did you know you had the same ideas on this? _____

## Getting along with brothers and sisters

"How can I get along with my sister when she doesn't even like me?" asked Lisa, age thirteen.

"I do too like you!" replied her sister Mary, fourteen. "Why do you think I don't like you?"

"Well, then, why are we always fighting?" asked Lisa tearfully.

"I don't know," replied Mary sadly, as tears started running down her face. "I just don't know."

It is not easy to live in a family where someone has a drinking problem. Brothers and sisters sometimes take problems and tensions out on each other by fighting or ignoring each other. This just makes everyone more lonely and unhappy. It doesn't have to be that way. Brothers and sisters can make living in a family more fun and less lonely. One way to do this is to understand and share feelings with each other.

Can you tell when your brother or sister is feeling mad or sad or hurt or happy? _____

How can you tell? _____

_____

What do they do or say that lets you know? _____

_____

Can you tell by looking at them? _____

_____

Write your name and the names of your brothers and sisters along the side. Then draw a picture or write in each box how you can tell they are having the feeling named at the top of the page. If you can't tell when they have that feeling, put an "X" in that box. Remember, you may have different answers for different brothers and sisters. (If you are an only child, you might want to do these exercises with your best friend in mind.)

## Family feelings

| NAME | HAPPY | MAD | SAD |
|---|---|---|---|
| Yours: | | | |
| | | | |
| | | | |
| | | | |

Which feelings seem easiest for you and your brothers and sisters to share?

_____

Which feelings are most difficult to share with your brothers and sisters?

_____

What do you want your brothers and sisters to do when you feel:

Happy? _____

Mad? _____

Sad? _____

Hurt? _____

Do your brothers and sisters know what you want them to do? _____

If not, can you ask them to do that? _____

Ask your brothers and sisters what they want <u>you</u> to do when <u>they</u> feel*:

Happy _____

Mad _____

Sad _____

Hurt _____

*You may have different answers from different brothers and sisters.

Do you think you can do what they want you to do when they have those

feelings? _____

In the boxes on the next page, write the names of your brothers and sisters (or

your best friend if you are an only child.) Then write what you like about them.

Write one box about yourself and what you like about you.

# What I like about . . .

| | |
|---|---|
| **Your name**<br><br><br><br><br> | **Name**<br><br><br><br><br> |
| **Name**<br><br><br><br><br> | **Name**<br><br><br><br><br> |

Have you ever told your brothers and sisters what you like about them?

What do you think would happen if you did? _____

_____

We all need to hear good things about ourselves. Try telling your brothers and sisters what you like about them. Here are some examples:

"Tom, thank you for fixing my bike."

"Mike, that shirt looks nice on you."

"Maureen, those cookies you baked tasted almost as good as Grandma's."

I like it when you _____

_____

I felt good when you _____

_____

Here are some other rules that might help you get along with your brothers and sisters*:

1. Always ask permission to borrow things <u>before</u> you borrow them.

2. Take good care of the things you borrow.

3. Don't tease.

4. Don't embarrass each other.

5. Spend time away from each other. Give each other privacy to do things alone or with other friends.

Can you think of some other rules that would help you and your brothers and sisters get along better?

Write them here: (You might want to ask your brothers and sisters for <u>their</u> suggestions.)

_____

_____

_____

Talk to your brothers and sisters about these rules. See if you can make an agreement to follow them.

*These rules were adapted from a good book called *Surviving Fights With Your Brothers And Sisters* © 1978 Joy Wilt, used by permission of Word Educational Products, Waco, Texas 76796. You might want to read this book with your brothers and sisters.

## Having an alcoholic brother or sister

Up until now we have talked mostly about living with a parent who drinks too much. It's not always a parent who is the alcoholic in the family. Sometimes it is a brother or sister who has a drinking or drug problem.

Dan, age twelve, has an older brother Tim, sixteen, who has a drinking problem. "My mom and dad are always worrying about Tim," says Dan. "They are so busy worrying about him and his drinking that they forget about me. I got good grades and I made the basketball team, but they hardly noticed. I try to do everything right, but <u>he</u> gets most of the attention. It makes me mad!"

If you have an alcoholic or drug-using brother or sister, do you feel like Dan?

_____

What do you do with those feelings when you feel like that?

_____

You might try to talk to your mom and dad about your feelings. They probably don't realize how you feel. Tell them. Ask them to spend some time just with you.

It is very difficult for parents to have a son or daughter who is alcoholic. Parents often feel very worried or guilty. They may be very strict with you because they don't want the same thing to happen again. They may spend much of their time worrying about the alcoholic or drug-using son or daughter. Maybe this makes you think they have forgotten about you. It is important for you to talk with your parents so you can understand each other's feelings.

Many kids with alcoholic brothers and sisters have some of the same confusing feelings that kids with alcoholic parents have. Paul has an alcoholic sister, Susan. He feels so angry at his sister for the trouble she has caused in the family. "I feel scared, too," he said. "Sometimes the police will call my dad to come get my sister out of jail or

33

from the hospital. My dad gets so upset that I'm afraid he'll have an accident on the way. And my mom cries and feels so ashamed. It makes me <u>so mad at Susan</u>!

Paul also said "I always feel as if I have to be extra good to make up for all the trouble my sister causes my parents. I try to make really good grades and do lots of chores around the house. I try really hard, but I just can't seem to make up to my parents for all the worry Susan causes them."

If you have an alcoholic brother or sister, do you ever feel the way that Paul does? _____

No matter what you do, you can't take away your parents' pain and sadness about your alcoholic or drug-dependent brother or sister. You can't make it up to them. Your job is to do the best <u>you</u> can to grow and learn and enjoy <u>your</u> life. That's the best thing you can do for yourself and your parents.

## One more time, since these are important to remember:

1. All families have problems. Learning to handle problems in a good way helps family members to grow and to be closer to each other.

2. Most of the time it helps to talk to someone you trust about your confusing feelings.

3. Brothers and sisters can help each other by listening and trying to understand each other's feelings.

4. If you have an alcoholic brother or sister, you probably have some confusing feelings. You may want to talk with your mom and dad about your feelings.

# 4
# Coping with Problems

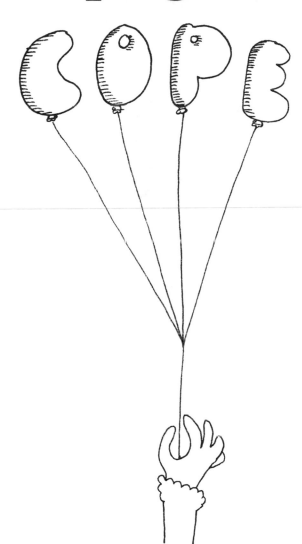

COPE is an important word. To cope with a problem means to handle the problem in a good way. Coping with a problem won't always make it go away. Coping with a problem will make it easier to live with.

When you read this book and do these exercises, you are learning to cope with your family's problems. You are showing that you care about yourself and your family.

This chapter talks about problems that kids sometimes have while they are living in a family where drinking is causing trouble. Here are some suggestions for coping with these problems. You may have other suggestions. Write them on the lines below the problem.

PROBLEM: When you feel unloved and lonely...

John's dad is an alcoholic. He doesn't live with John and his mom anymore. Since John's dad left, John's mom always seems too busy or too tired to pay much attention to John. She is always worrying about the bills and the housework. She is sad or crabby much of the time. John feels abandoned by his dad. He feels like a burden to his mother. He refuses to pick up his room or do his chores. He won't do his homework anymore. He and his mom yell at each other. John feels hurt and angry and lonely. He feels as though his parents don't love him anymore.

SUGGESTION: It might help for John and his mom to talk about their feelings with each other. John's mom probably doesn't want to forget about John. She probably doesn't know how hurt and angry John feels. She is so busy coping with her own problems, she may need to be reminded about John's problems. It might help if John could ask for what he needs: "I know you are worried and busy, Mom, but I feel hurt and lonely when dad left and you forget about me. Sometimes I need a hug so that I know you still love me. Can I have a hug?"

Also, John could show his mom that he respects her feelings .by doing his chores and cleaning his room. John's mom might be more willing to spend time with John if he helps her.

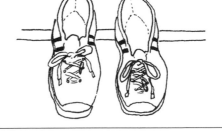

YOUR SUGGESTION: _____

_____

_____

_____

PROBLEM: Feeling "in the middle."

Jack's mom is an alcoholic. His parents are divorced. Since his mom can't take care of Jack, Jack lives with his dad. Jack's dad is still very angry with Jack's mom. He says hurtful, angry things about Mom, whom Jack still loves. Jack feels like he should defend his mom to his dad. He and Dad end up arguing.

SUGGESTION: Jack's dad is still feeling hurt and angry about the divorce and the drinking. He says hurtful, angry things because he hasn't been able to cope with his feelings. Jack understands that his mom is sick with alcoholism. He still loves her though. He loves his dad, too. And that is okay. After all, even if Jack's parents are divorced, they are still his parents. He cares about both of them. But he doesn't need to listen to them cut each other down. Jack could say to his dad, 'I know you have angry and hurt feelings about mom. But when you keep saying terrible things about her, I feel sad. You are both my parents and I care about both of you. I know Mom has lots of problems, but please don't keep telling me all the bad things about her. Can we please talk about something else?"

YOUR SUGGESTION: _____

_____

_____

_____

PROBLEM: Parents fighting.

Night after night Ricky, ten, hears his parents fighting. He listens and tries to figure out who is right and who is wrong. When he listens to them, he feels scared and his stomach hurts.

SUGGESTION: Kids can't solve their parents' problems. Trying to figure out parents' fights is a waste of time. You only end up feeling bad. When parents fight, it is best to go somewhere where you can't hear. Try going to your friend's house, or to watch TV. If you have a brother or sister, you might want to spend time with each other. You can help each other feel better.

YOUR SUGGESTION: _____

_____

_____

_____

PROBLEM: A parent has been drinking and is going to drive you somewhere. Mark's mom comes to pick him up after school. Mark can tell that she has been drinking. He's afraid to ride home with her.

SUGGESTION: If possible, have a plan worked out ahead of time with your other parent or another adult. Let that person know that you are worried about the drinking and driving. Carry

with you the phone number of where you can call your sober parent (or a neighbor) to give you a ride home. Or you can ask your teacher or counselor to give you a ride. Or call the police. Tell them your problem and ask them for a ride home. Remember: You have a right to feel safe. It is okay to tell your drinking parent that you don't want to ride with him or her.

YOUR SUGGESTION: _____

_____

_____

PROBLEM: You are afraid to ask your friends over because your mom or dad might get drunk and embarrass you.

Randy had been at his friend Joe's house several times for dinner. Randy felt he should invite Joe to his house, but Randy worried that it would be one of the days his mom would get drunk and forget to fix dinner.

SUGGESTION: You might discuss the problem with your non-drinking parent. Maybe you can come up with another plan, such as taking your friend to dinner at the drive-in or pizza place. Or perhaps your non-drinking parent can promise to be home to help you prepare the meal and supervise the situation.

YOUR SUGGESTION: _____

_____

_____

PROBLEM: Some kids at school call your parent a drunk. You feel so embarrassed you just want to hide.

SUGGESTION: It's natural for kids to want to be proud of their parents, and embarrassing when other kids tease or call names. But remember whose problem the drinking is—your parent's, not yours.

Also remember that alcoholism is a disease. Your parent isn't trying to embarrass you on purpose. Try to keep your cool and ignore the kids' remarks. If they are good friends of yours, you may want to explain about alcoholism to them. Or maybe you can show them this workbook or one of the books about alcoholism listed in the back of this book.

YOUR SUGGESTION: _____

_____

_____

_____

PROBLEM: You want to feel better and you think drinking might help.

Janet's family had so many problems that they seemed to forget about her. She felt neglected and lonely and worried. She would watch her dad drink and it seemed to make him laugh and feel silly. She wanted to feel good, too. She thought about sneaking some of her dad's beer.

SUGGESTION: Some kids try to feel better by drinking or using drugs. This is not a good way to try to feel better. They could end up addicted too. They could become alcoholic. A better way to handle lonely, left-out feelings is to let somebody

40

know your feelings. Tell your friend, parent, brother, or sister, that you are feeling lonely. You might want to ask for a hug. Or ask that person to do something with you, like go for a walk or play a game. Or you might write a letter to a friend. These are better ways to cope with lonely and worried feelings.

YOUR SUGGESTION: _____

_____

_____

_____

PROBLEM: Your parents expect you to be perfect...

Susan's mom expects her to be perfect. Whenever Susan makes a mistake, like forgetting her books at school or burning the toast, her mom gets very angry. She says Susan is stupid and careless. Susan thinks she can never be good enough to please her mom. That makes Susan feel sad and frustrated and angry.

SUGGESTION: Sometimes parents expect children to be perfect because they (parents) can't accept that they aren't perfect themselves. They are angry and frustrated themselves, but they take it out on their children.

Remind yourself that no one can be perfect. Everyone makes mistakes. It is enough to do the best you can.

YOUR SUGGESTION: _____           _____

_____

_____

_____

PROBLEM: A parent gets angry and loses control...

Eric forgot to put his bike away in the garage. Eric's dad came home drunk. He saw the bike, and got very angry at Eric. He started yelling and hitting Eric across the face and back.

SUGGESTION: Sometimes parents lose control of themselves, especially when they are drunk. No child deserves to be hurt. If your parent loses control — or is about to — go to a neighbor's or call the police. If you are hit or abused, always be sure to tell a teacher, counselor, school nurse, or neighbor who can help you and perhaps help your parent too. Or you can call for help yourself. To get help right away, call the police. Write the emergency number here:

Every state has offices that are in charge of protecting children and getting help for parents who hurt their kids. Write the telephone number for the child abuse hotline here: _____ .

YOUR SUGGESTION: _____

_____

_____

_____

PROBLEM: You are touched in a way that you don't want to be touched.

Angie's dad got very drunk. He started touching her under her pajamas, all over her body, including her private parts. Angie did not like this. She was very scared. She did not know what to do.

SUGGESTION: Your body belongs to you. No one has a right to touch it without your permission. If someone is touching your private parts, you should try to pull away and call for help. If the person is too big and too drunk, you might not be able to get help right away. But you should tell someone as soon as possible. You could tell a teacher, a counselor, the school nurse, or your non-drinking parent. If the person you tell doesn't do anything right away, you should tell another adult who could help you. You can also call the number listed under the last problem.

YOUR SUGGESTION: _____

_____

_____

_____

What are some other problems that kids in alcoholic families have? Write them here:

PROBLEM: _____

_____

_____

SUGGESTION: _____

_____

_____

_____

PROBLEM: _____

_____

_____

_____

SUGGESTION: _____

_____

_____

_____

## One more time, since these are important to remember:

1. Every family has problems. Learning to handle problems in a good way is called "coping" with a problem.

2. When parents are fighting, it is best to go someplace where you cannot hear them. You cannot solve your parents' fights. That's not your job.

3. You can't be perfect. Just do the best you can. That is good enough.

4. When you need something (like a hug or attention), ask for it. No one can read your mind.

5. If your parent loses control of anger and hurts you, tell someone (teacher, school nurse, grandparent).

6. Your body is yours, no one has a right to touch it if you don't want to be touched.

7. When you feel lonely, let somebody know. Ask for a hug or ask to do something together. This is a good way to handle lonely feelings. Drinking or using other drugs is not a good way to handle lonely feelings.

Suggested Reading:
   *Living With a Parent Who Drinks Too Much* by Judith Seixas.

# 5
# Changes

What would you like to change about your family? _____

_____

_____

_____

How would you make this happen? _____

_____

_____

_____

There are some things in our lives that we can change. There are other things we can't change even if we want to very much. It is a good idea to sort out which ones we can change and which ones we can't. Then we can work on changing the things we can, and not worry about the things we can't change.

Can <u>you</u> change what you wrote about above? _____

Sometimes we try very hard to control and change other people. I used to try to control my Dad's drinking. I'd fix him a drink and "forget" on purpose to put the alcohol in it. I put the drink in a colored glass so he couldn't see the difference. He always found out anyway. Then he went and made his own drink. I just could not stop him from drinking when he wanted to.

Did you ever try to keep your parent (or brother or sister) from drinking? _____

What happened? _____

_____

_____

No one can control another person's drinking. You can try, but it doesn't work for very long. You can't make someone an alcoholic. You can't make someone stop drinking, either.

## Taking care of yourself

Trying to control an alcoholic's drinking is a waste of energy. That energy you can use for other important things — like taking care of yourself and enjoying your own life. What can you do that makes you feel good? Make a list below of things you like to do:

_____  _____  _____

_____  _____  _____

_____  _____  _____

_____  _____  _____

_____  _____  _____

_____  _____  _____

_____  _____  _____

You are taking good care of yourself when you do something to make yourself feel good (as long as it doesn't hurt you or anyone else). This is one way of changing the things you can change in your life.

Sometimes we waste a lot of time and energy worrying about things we have no control over. This just makes us more frustrated and unhappy.

My mom had a friend who used to worry a lot about things she couldn't change. She decided she needed to help herself quit worrying so much. She took a cardboard box and cut a slot in the top. She named the box her "God Box." Whenever she started worrying about something she could not change, she wrote it down on a piece of paper. Then she folded it up and stuck it in her God Box. She'd say a prayer and then let God handle that worry. Putting the worry in the God Box made her feel better. It reminded her that she could not change these things. It also gave her more time to work on changing the things she could change.

Try this...

If you wish to, add endings to any of these sentences:

1. What I worry about most is _____

   _____

   - - - - - - - - - - - - - - - - - - - - - - - - - - - - - - - - - - - - - - - - - - - - - - - - -

2. Sometimes I'm afraid _____

   _____

   - - - - - - - - - - - - - - - - - - - - - - - - - - - - - - - - - - - - - - - - - - - - - - - - -

3. Sometimes I worry about Mom because _____

   _____

   - - - - - - - - - - - - - - - - - - - - - - - - - - - - - - - - - - - - - - - - - - - - - - - - -

4. Sometimes I worry about Dad because _____

   _____

   - - - - - - - - - - - - - - - - - - - - - - - - - - - - - - - - - - - - - - - - - - - - - - - - -

5. Sometimes I worry about _____ because
   (Name)

   - - - - - - - - - - - - - - - - - - - - - - - - - - - - - - - - - - - - - - - - - - - - - - - - -

   _____

6. Sometimes I worry about _____ because
   (Name)

   _____

- - - - - - - - - - - - - - - - - - - - - - - - - - - - - - - - - - - - - -

7. Sometimes I worry I _____

   _____

- - - - - - - - - - - - - - - - - - - - - - - - - - - - - - - - - - - - - -

8. Sometimes I worry that my friends _____

   _____

- - - - - - - - - - - - - - - - - - - - - - - - - - - - - - - - - - - - - -

9. Sometimes I worry about school because _____

   _____

- - - - - - - - - - - - - - - - - - - - - - - - - - - - - - - - - - - - - -

10. Other things I worry about are: _____

    _____

    _____

    _____

    _____

Which of these worries can <u>you</u> do something to change (make better)? Circle their numbers.

Which worries are ones you can't do much about? Write their numbers here:

_____

(Maybe you would like to make your own "God Box". Then you can cut those worries on the dotted line and put them in your box.)

## Worrying about things that haven't happened yet

Tessa, age ten, hears her parents fighting a lot. She worries that they might get a divorce. What do you think Tessa should do? _____

_____

_____

_____

_____

Can Tessa keep her parents from fighting? _____

Can Tessa keep her parents from getting a divorce if they really want one? ____

It is usually a good idea to try not to worry about things that haven't happened yet. Why? _____

1. They might never happen. Then you did all that worrying for nothing. You can waste a lot of energy worrying about things that have not happened yet.

2. If they do happen, you can cope with them then. You'll probably have more energy to cope because you haven't wasted it all on worrying.

## Handling uncomfortable feelings

Sometimes we want most of all to change our uncomfortable feelings. Charlie's dad stopped drinking three months ago. Charlie's family has been seeing a counselor, and Charlie's dad goes to AA. Charlie still feels hurt and very angry about some of the things his dad did while he was drinking. Charlie sometimes feels like he's walking around with a bag on his back, stuffed full with hurt and anger. It makes him uncomfortable to hang onto so many bad feelings, but he doesn't know what to do with them.

Did you ever feel like Charlie? _____

What feelings are stuck in your bag?

Sometimes if we keep hurt and angry feelings inside, they seem to harden like cement. Have you ever tried carrying around a bag of cement? It gets heavy. You don't have much energy to do anything else. Holding on to hurt and angry feelings can drain your energy, too.

So what can you do when you have lots of hurt and angry feelings like Charlie's? In chapter two we talked about recognizing and accepting your feelings. But that doesn't mean you have to hold on to them and carry them around forever. Sometimes it is best just to let the bad memories and feelings float up to the top, then let them go. Don't hang on to them. Get busy thinking and doing other things that help you take care of yourself and make you feel good about yourself. You don't have to be dragged down by bad feelings.

There is something else you can do to keep from being dragged down by all those bad memories and uncomfortable feelings. You can forgive the person.

"How can I forgive my dad?" asked Charlie. "No matter how hard I try, I can't forget some of the hurts he did to me and my mom when he was drinking."

Some things are hard to forget. But you don't have to forget to forgive. Just try to let the bad feelings float up to the top and let them go. Don't hang on to them.

Charlie's dad hurt and embarrassed Charlie and his mom by many of the things he did when he was drinking. Charlie feels very angry. Charlie can decide he will be angry with his dad forever if he wants to. Or Charlie can decide to give his dad another chance. He can let his dad know how glad he is that his dad stopped drinking. Maybe Charlie and his dad can try to make a better relationship. Can you think of someone you would like to forgive? _____

Another good thing to remember is that although some changes happen quickly, other changes take more time. It's important for Charlie and his dad to accept that everything isn't going to be better right away. Charlie will need some time to learn to trust his dad again. His dad will need time, too, to learn new ways of living and handling his feelings without drinking. Some days will be better than other days. Both Charlie and his dad will need to be patient with each other as they adjust to these new changes. If they can be patient and keep trying to live just one day at a time, things can get better and better. (I know it's possible because now my dad is one of my very best friends!)

There is a good prayer that people in AA, Al-Anon and Alateen say:

"God grant me the serenity

to accept the things I cannot change,

the courage to change the things I can,

and the wisdom to know the difference."

(grant means give; serenity means peace)

## Your changes

Think about yourself and your life. What are some things you can change by yourself? What are some things you could change if you had some help from somebody else? What are some things that you can't change, no mattter how hard you try?

Things I can change myself:

_____

_____

_____

_____

Things I could change if I had some help:

_____

_____

_____

_____

Things I can't change:

_____

_____

_____

_____

_____

## One more time, since these are important:

1. Some things about our life we can change. Other things we can't.

2. We can't make other people change, we can't control someone's drinking.

3. We can change ourselves. We can do things to take care of ourselves and make ourselves happy.

4. We should try not to worry about things we can't change or about things that haven't happened yet.

5. Try not to hang onto hurt and angry feelings. Let them float through, or share them with a close friend or counselor.

6. Even if you can't forget, you can forgive.

7. After an alcoholic quits drinking, everything doesn't get better right away. It takes time to learn new ways to handle feelings. It takes time to learn to trust.

# 6
# Choices

Pete ran to catch up with his friend Matt one day after school. "Matt, congratulations on making the Number One spot on the wrestling team. I'm glad somebody finally beat that Joe. He's always walking around with such a big head. Maybe now he won't act like such a big shot."

"Shhh!," said Matt. "There's Joe up ahead."

Pete saw Joe and several of his friends waiting at the corner. Joe was leaning against the light post chewing on a blade of grass. "Hey, Matt," he said, "I saw your dad last night at the bowling alley. He was so drunk, he threw his ball down the wrong lane."

Joe continued, "But that wasn't nearly as funny as the time your dad came to church so drunk he fell over his own feet trying to pass the collection plate!"

Dark clouds of anger flashed in Matt's eyes.

Joe turned to the other guys. "Let's see how the drunk's kid can fight without some wrestling coach and mats around. With both fists made, Joe stepped up to Matt. "Now we'll see who's the real man."

Matt's whole body stiffened with anger. He clenched his fists. He was about to hit Joe, then stopped. He dropped his arms. Looking Joe straight in the eye, he said, "I'm more a man than you'll ever be." Then Matt turned to Pete, "Let's go." He walked off down the street.

Pete rushed to catch up with Matt. "Hey, what's the matter with you, Matt? You could have laid him out flat. Why'd you walk away? Now they'll say you're a real sissy."

Matt kept walking for several blocks. Finally, he stopped and looked at Pete. "I'm not taking anything, Pete. I've known for a long time that my dad's got a drinking problem. In fact, I've been going to these meetings called Alateen. They are for kids who have an alcoholic parent. I've been learning some good stuff there. One thing I've learned is that I don't have to stand around just reacting to everybody else. I can choose how I'm going to act. And I choose not to bruise my knuckles on a jerk like Joe!"

What would you do if somebody called your parent a drunk? How would you choose to act? _____

_____

We don't always get to choose what happens to us, but we can choose how we react to what happens to us.

Every day of our lives we make choices. Listed below are some choices you might make in a day. Put a circle around the choices you made today. You can add your own too:

      What food to eat for breakfast
      What clothes to wear
      Which friend(s) to play with
      What TV show to watch
      Which feeling to share with others
      Which feeling to keep to myself
      Which games to play

_____

_____

_____

As you grow up, you'll make even more choices. Some of the choices you make might be:

      What kind of work you want to do
      How you want to spend your money
      If you want to buy a car and what kind
      If you want to get married or not

Whom you want to marry

If you want to have children and how many

Whether or not you want to drink or use drugs

Making decisions (choices) is one of the best parts of being a person — and also one of the most difficult. Learning how to make good decisions is very important. Good decisions are ones which help you take good care of yourself. Put a circle around the decisions that show you are taking good care of yourself:

- You eat so much candy that you get sick to your stomach.

- You have a cold so you decide to go to bed early.

- You feel lonely so you decide to call your friend on the phone.

- You want to be liked by your friend. He asks you to shoplift. You do.

Good decisions are decisions that show you respect and care about other people, too. Put a circle around the decisions that show you care about the other person:

- You want to borrow your sister's bike. First you ask her if that is okay.

- You told your brother that you would help him with his homework. Then your friend calls and asks you to go to the movies with his family. You decide to go to the movies instead of helping your brother.

- The shortest way to get to school is to cut through your neighbor's garden. It's impossible to get through the garden without stepping on the plants. You're in a hurry, so you cut through the garden.

- Everybody is putting down the new kid in the class. You think he's okay. You say so to the others.

Here are six steps to making a good decision. These steps come from a book called *Making Up Your Own Mind* © 1978 Joy Wilt, used by permission of Word Educational Products, Waco, Texas 76796. You might want to read this book yourself.

Step One:      Determine what needs to be decided.

Step Two:      Determine what the choices are.

Step Three:    Think about the choices.

Step Four:     Choose the best alternative.

Step Five:      Do what you have decided to do.

Step Six:      Think back over your decision.

In this example, use these same steps to help Tom make a good decision.

Tom is twelve years old. His parents just recently got divorced. Tom's dad is an alcoholic and can't take care of Tom, so Tom lives with his mom. Because his mom just got a new job in a different city, they moved and Tom is new at school. He's lonely and wants to make friends. Paul, one of the kids in his class, invites Tom and several other guys to his house one day after school. Paul's parents aren't home. Paul and his friends decide to drink some of Paul's dad's beer. They encourage Tom to have some, too. Tom wants very much to be accepted by Paul and his friends. But Tom also knows the trouble alcohol can cause. He knows it is against the law for kids his age to drink alcohol. Still, Tom is nervous and he notices that the guys relax as they drink more beer. He would like to feel more relaxed...

Using the steps for good decision-making, help Tom decide what to do.

Step One: What needs to be decided? _____

_____

Step Two: What are Tom's choices? _____

_____

Step Three: Think about the choices. What might happen if Tom decides to drink

the beer? _____

_____

What might happen if Tom decides not to drink the beer? _____

_____

Which decision would show that Tom is taking good care of himself? _____

_____

Which decision would show that Tom respects other people? _____

_____

Which decision will help Tom be the kind of person he wants to be in the future?

_____

Make a plus (+) and minus (−) chart for each decision. Put the good things that would happen because of that choice on the + side. Put the bad things that would happen on the − side.

Tom decides to drink the beer.

| + | − |
|---|---|
|   |   |
|   |   |
|   |   |
|   |   |

Tom decides <u>not</u> to drink the beer.

| + | − |
|---|---|
|   |   |
|   |   |
|   |   |
|   |   |

<u>Step Four</u>: Choose the best alternative. Circle it.

Tom decides to drink the beer.

Tom decides <u>not</u> to drink the beer.

<u>Step Five</u>: Tom does what he decided to do.

Step Six: Think back over the decision. What do you think happened?

_____

_____

_____

Do you think it was a good decision? _____

_____

_____

Think of a decision you have to make about a problem that you have. Use the decision-making steps to help you make a decision.

Step One: What needs to be decided? _____

_____

Step Two: What are your choices? (Ask your group or other friends or family members to help you think up choices.):

1. _____

_____

2. _____

_____

3. _____

_____

4. _____

_____

Step Three: Think about your choices. What do you think would happen as a result of each choice?

1. _____

_____

2. _____

_____

3. _____

_____

4. _____

_____

Step Four: Choose the best alternative. The best choice for me is number _____

Step Five: Do what you have decided to do.

Step Six: Think back over your decision.

## Thinking about drinking

Someday you will need to decide whether or not you want to use alcohol and other drugs. It's an important decision. It is an especially important decision if someone in your family is an alcoholic.

As was said in chapter one, alcoholism seems to run in some families. Scientists and doctors have not yet figured out why this is. Maybe some people's bodies react differently to alcohol and other drugs. Maybe this makes it easier to become addicted (stuck). Or maybe because if some people grow up watching a parent use alcohol to cope with uncomfortable feelings, they too learn to drink to hide uncomfortable feelings too. Then they can become addicted.

Also, children who grow up with an alcoholic in the family sometimes marry an alcoholic. Why? Nobody knows for sure why that is — maybe because people often marry people like their parents.

Does this mean that you will grow up to be alcoholic or marry an alcoholic?

No. It does not mean you have to grow up to be alcoholic or marry an alcoholic. It can be different for you, especially if you learn a better way of living. This book is a start.

I remember when I was younger, I told myself I would NEVER become stuck on alcohol like my dad was. I told myself I would NEVER marry an alcoholic like my mom had done. If I ever got married, I would NEVER scream and yell like they did. I grew up and moved away from home. My dad's drinking kept getting worse. Finally, he decided to get help. I went to visit him at the special hospital where he was staying so that he could get help for his alcoholism. I went to lectures, saw films, and talked in groups with counselors and other people about this disease of alcoholism. I took a close look at my own drinking and relationships with other people. I did not like what I saw. I realized I might be on my way to being stuck too. I was starting to drink to get rid of my uncomfortable feelings. I realized the man I dated had a drinking problem. Sometimes we yelled at each other the way I said I never would. I certainly wasn't taking very good care of myself. I was not the person I wanted to be.

When I realized all of this, I was very angry with myself. How could I have let this happen to me? I thought I knew better. Finally I calmed down and thought about the situation reasonably. I realized that my situation couldn't be different for me unless I <u>learned</u> a new way. If I wanted to stop drinking as a way of handling uncomfortable feelings, then I would need to learn a better way to handle feelings. If I wanted to be able to express my anger without screaming and yelling, I would have to <u>learn</u> how to express anger differently. If I didn't want an alcoholic husband, then I'd better stop dating a man with a drinking problem. I needed to learn to take better care of myself.

Now I am learning to take better care of myself, along with better ways to handle my feelings. But these new ways weren't easy to learn. And I didn't learn them by myself. I got lots of help from my friends, my family, counselors, and other people who were coping with problems like mine. I found help in books like this one. And somewhere in the middle of all those people, books, and situations, I think God was there too. I was definitely not alone, even when I felt alone.

You are not alone, either. There are people in the world who can and will help you in your life. Whether you decide to drink or not to drink, find people you can share your feelings and your problems with. Ask for what you need. Although there probably is no one person who can help you with everything, different people can help with different things. Make a list below of the people you can ask for help when you need it. There are lots of helpers around. Think about your friends, parents, brothers, sisters, neighbors, teachers, counselors, ministers, coaches, Scout leaders.

**If I needed...**                                        **I could ask...**

    help with my homework                 _____

    a hug                                  _____

    to talk about my hurt feelings         _____

    to talk to someone when I feel lonely  _____

someone to play a game or watch TV with  _____

_____          _____

_____          _____

_____          _____

Remember: There <u>are</u> people around to help. You need to ask so they know you want help. If you don't find someone right away, keep looking and asking.

If you stop to think about it, you already have much of what it takes to be close to other people and to take care of yourself.

To help you remember good things about yourself, try this. Take a blank piece of paper. Write your name in big letters on the paper. Then use tape to stick it on your back with your name showing. Give crayons to the other kids in your group. You can do this at home with your family too. Have them write words (or draw pictures), telling what they like about you. Meanwhile you write what you like about them on their backs. Don't worry about spelling. Here are some words you might want to use:

| funny | helps people | handsome |
|-------|-------------|----------|
| nice | kind | understanding |
| shares feelings | honest | good at sports |
| pretty | sings well | has nice eyes |

When everyone is finished, take the paper off your back and read it. You may want to save it. Sometime when you have a bad day, you can take it out to read and make yourself feel better.

## One more time, since these are important:

1.  We don't always get to choose what happens to us, but we do get to choose how we <u>react</u> to what happens.

2.  Making choices is one of the best, but also one of the most difficult, parts of being a person.

3.  Good decisions are decisions that show respect for yourself and other people.

4.  You don't have to be limited by what happened in the past. You don't have to grow up to be an alcoholic or marry one.

5.  If you want things to be different for you, you have to learn new ways to act and to handle feelings.

6.  You don't have to do things alone. There are people around who can help you. You need to find them and ask them to help.

7.  You can be close to other people. You can grow up to be the kind of person you want to be.

# The end
# or the beginning?

I hope this book, and the people you've shared it with, will be of help to you as you learn new ways to become the person you want to be. May your future be interesting and happy!

Jill Hastings

# Suggested reading

Other books you might want to read:

Black, Claudia. *My Dad Loves Me, My Dad Has A Disease*. ACT, 1979. (Alcoholism Children's Therapy).

Brooks, Cathleen. *The Secret Everyone Knows*. Available from Operation Cork, 8939 Villa LaJolla Drive, San Diego, CA 92037. 1981.

LeShan, Eda. *What Makes Me Feel This Way?: Growing Up With Human Emotions*. Collier Books, New York. 1972.

Seixas, Judith. *Alcohol: What It Is, What It Does*. Greenwillow Books: William Morrow & Co., Inc., New York. 1977.

Seixas, Judith. *Living With a Parent Who Drinks Too Much*. Greenwillow Books: William Morrow & Co., Inc., New York. 1979.

Snyder, Anne. *First Step*. Holt, Rinehart, and Winston, New York. 1975.

Snyder, Anne. *Kids and Drinking*. CompCare Publishers. Minneapolis. 1977.

Tobias, Ann. *Pot: What It Is, What It Does*. Greenwillow Books: William Morrow & Co., Inc. New York. 1975.

Wilt, Joy. *Handling Your Ups and Downs; Surviving Fights With Your Brothers and Sisters; Making Up Your Own Mind*. Three titles from Ready-Set-Grow series. Educational Products Division, Word, Inc., P.O. Box 1790, Waco, Texas 76796.

Many of these books are available from CompCare Publishers, 2415 Annapolis Lane, Minneapolis, Minnesota 55441.

# About the authors

Jill Hastings has earned her Ph.D. in Human Development and Family Studies from the University of Missouri, Columbia, where she also received her B.S. in Education—in Behavioral Sciences and Rehabilitation Services and her M.S. in Child and Family Development.

Jill's experience has included teaching, counseling, and curriculum development for the public school system in Columbia, and working with handicapped and disadvantaged adolescents and young adults in rehabilitation programs.

Currently, she is working as a child and family therapist at Youth and Shelter Services in Ames, Iowa. She also works as a counselor in the schools in Ames and coordinates and teaches drug prevention and education programs in the schools there.

Jill is a Clinical Member of the American Association of Marriage and Family Therapy. She is also a member of the American Association for Counseling and Development, American School Counselors Association, and the International Association of Marriage and Family Counseling.


Marion H. Typpo is Assistant Professor of Human Development and Family Studies at the University of Missouri in Columbia, where she teaches courses in adolescence and early adulthood, family development, adulthood and aging, and violence in the family. She holds a Ph.D. in Child and Family Development from the University of Missouri, an M.A. in Counseling and Psychology from the University of Minnesota in Minneapolis, and a B.A. in Psychology and Sociology from the University of Minnesota in Duluth.

Marion is a Board Member of McCambridge Center, a shelter for women who are victims of alcoholism and drug abuse. She is active in campus issues of alcoholism and abuse, serving on an advisory committee to work with students at the University of Missouri. She was asked to lead a workshop in Finland on women's issues and the impact of alcoholism in the family, focusing on women as caretakers. As a result of her involvement in that workshop, *An Elephant in the Living Room* is being used in a program near the Arctic Circle.

Her professional memberships include the American Psychological Association, National Council for Family Relations, American Association for Counseling and Development, and the Missouri Prevention Network.

Date _____

Please help us improve the groups by filling out this paper:

In group I learned _____

_____

_____

What I liked best about the group was _____

_____

_____

What I didn't like about the group was _____

_____

_____

I wish we could have _____

_____

_____

What I liked about the leader was _____

_____

_____

Any other suggestions or comments: _____

_____

_____

Will you help us improve this book? We would love to hear from you. Please fill out this letter, fold it, and mail to: Jill Hastings, CompCare Publishers, 2415 Annapolis Lane, Minneapolis, Minnesota 55441.

Dear Jill:

From this book I learned _____

_____

_____

What I liked best about the book was _____

_____

What I didn't like about the book was _____

_____

I wish this book had more _____

_____

The activities I liked best were _____

_____

The activities I liked least were _____

_____

Other suggestions to improve this book are _____

_____

_____

_____

_____

From:

Place
Stamp
Here

Jill Hastings
CompCare Publishers
2415 Annapolis Lane
Minneapolis, MN 55441

I, _____, on _____
          (Name)                              (Date)

finished reading

## An Elephant in the Living Room.

I am learning to
   feel all my feelings;
   share my feelings if I want to;
   ask for help and attention when I need it:
   tell the difference between things I can change and things
   I can not change;
   do the best I can, and not worry about being perfect;
   forgive people who hurt me or my feelings;
   make decisions that are good for me;
   cope with my problems;
   have fun and do things that make me feel good about myself
   What else? _____
   _____
   _____
   _____

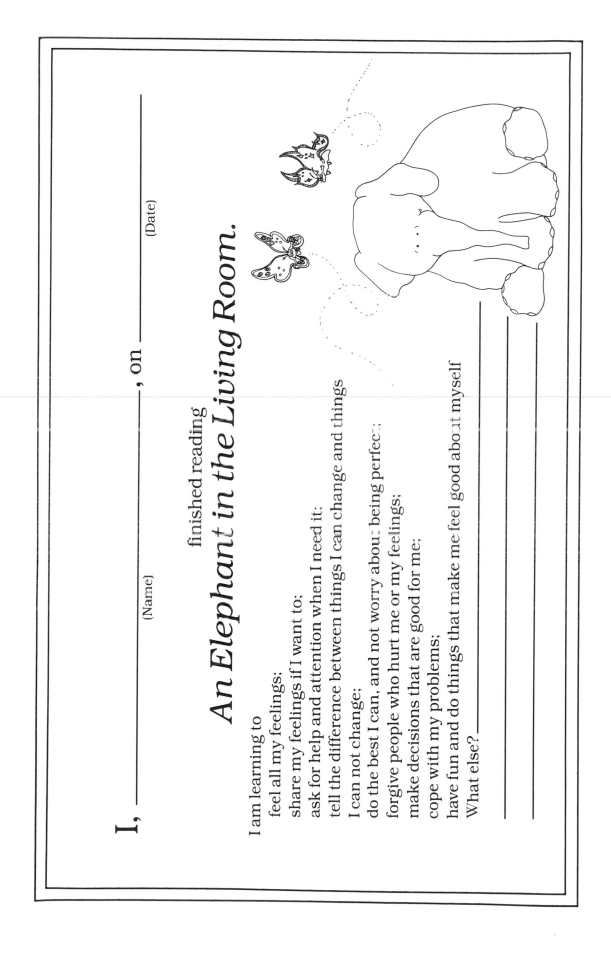